More HYMN CREATIONS

10 PIANO SOLO ARRANGEMENTS

by Randall Hartsell

ISBN 978-1-4803-5584-2

WILLIS MUSIC

EXCLUSIVELY DISTRIBUTED BY

HAL•LEONARD®
CORPORATION

7777 W. BLUEMOUND RD. P.O. BOX 13819 MILWAUKEE, WI 53213

Visit Hal Leonard Online at
www.halleonard.com

PREFACE

Church music traditions run deep in my family heritage. I grew up in a small North Carolina community, and church gave me numerous musical opportunities such as singing in choirs and performing my original compositions on the piano for an audience. This collection contains many familiar hymns from this early part of my life.

As in my original *Hymn Creations* collection, these arrangements come from an improvisatory style and are often used with my own congregation. Many of these arrangements are lyrical and utilize *rubato* and fresh harmonic sounds. However, I always strived to maintain the integrity of the traditional hymns. The music works well as preludes and postludes in worship settings and as quiet music for reflective parts of church services, but they can also be useful as teaching pieces. Some of these arrangements have bold dynamic changes and strong-sounding chords to inspire strength and courage in the listener.

Feel free to adapt this music creatively into your worship environment and into your teaching for use. Hearing these beautiful hymn tunes with fresh ears may help to keep these tunes alive for another generation.

Randall Hartsell

CONTENTS

All Things Bright and Beautiful

Words by Cecil Frances Alexander
17th Century English Melody
Arranged by Randall Hartsell

Quickly, lightly

With pedal

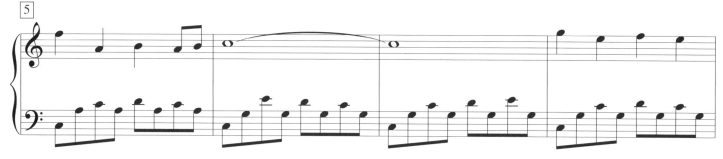

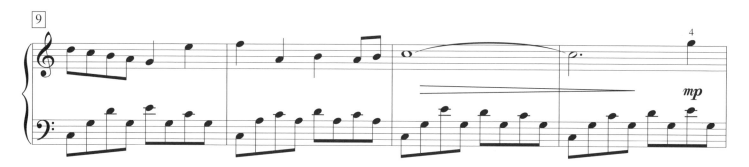

cresc. poco a poco

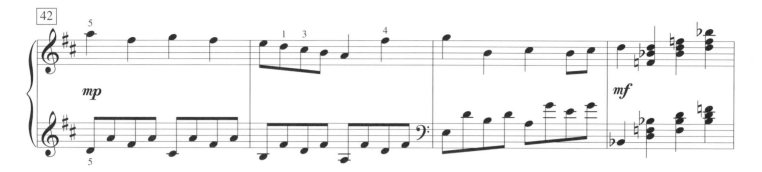

Blessed Assurance

Lyrics by Fanny J. Crosby
Music by Phoebe Palmer Knapp
Arranged by Randall Hartsell

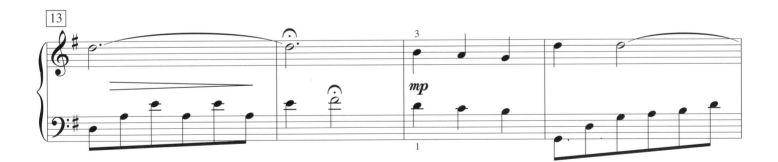

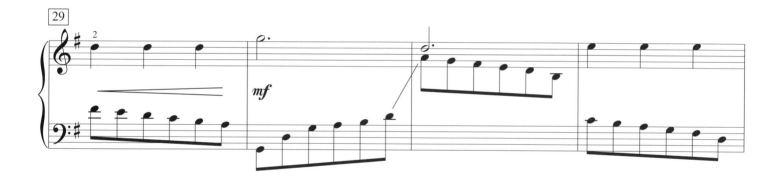

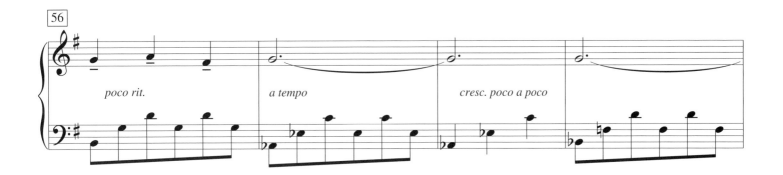

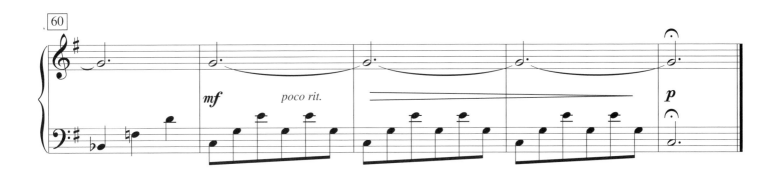

Break Thou the Bread of Life

Words by Mary Artemesia Lathbury
Music by William Fiske Sherwin
Arranged by Randall Hartsell

Come, Thou Almighty King

Traditional
Music by Felice de Giardini
Arranged by Randall Hartsell

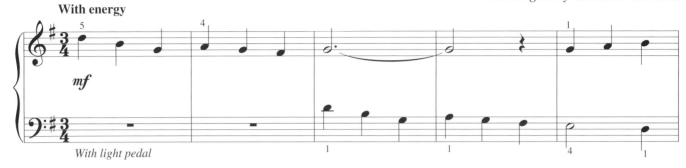

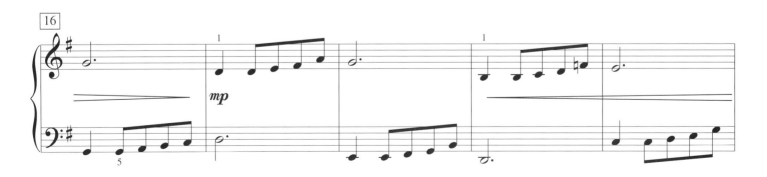

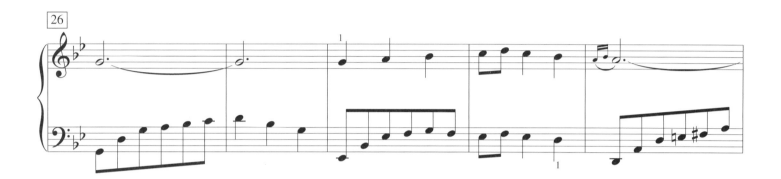

Glorious Things of Thee Are Spoken

Words by John Newton
Music by Franz Joseph Haydn
Arranged by Randall Hartsell

He Leadeth Me

Words by Joseph H. Gilmore
Music by William B. Bradbury
Arranged by Randall Hartsell

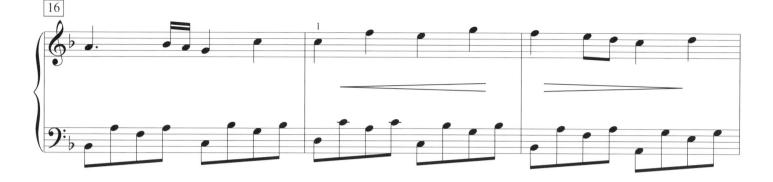

Immortal, Invisible

Words by Walter Chalmers Smith
Traditional Welsh Melody
Arranged by Randall Hartsell

Jesus, the Very Thought of Thee

Words attributed to Bernard of Clairvaux
Translated by Edward Caswall
Music by John Bacchus Dykes
Arranged by Randall Hartsell

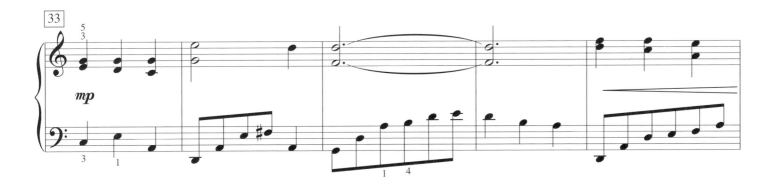

My Hope Is Built on Nothing Less

Words by Edward Mote
Music by John B. Dykes
Arranged by Randall Hartsell

Majestically

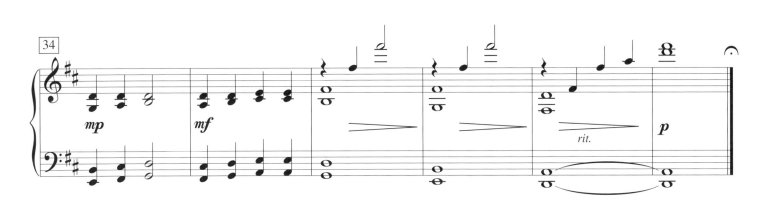

'Tis So Sweet to Trust in Jesus

Words by Louisa M.R. Stead
Music by William J. Kirkpatrick
Arranged by Randall Hartsell

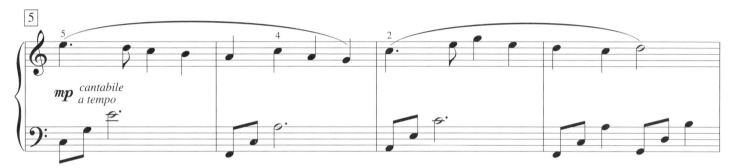

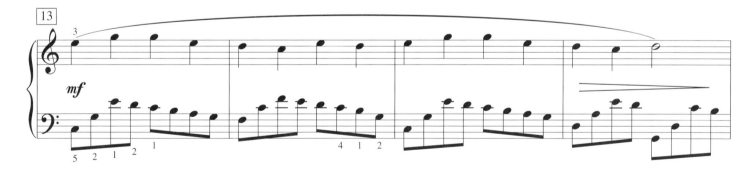

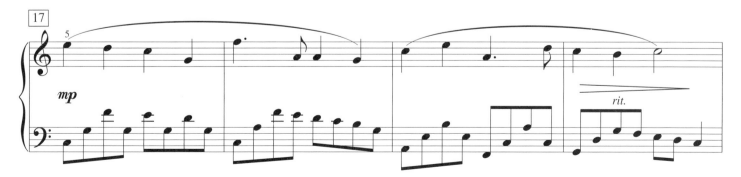

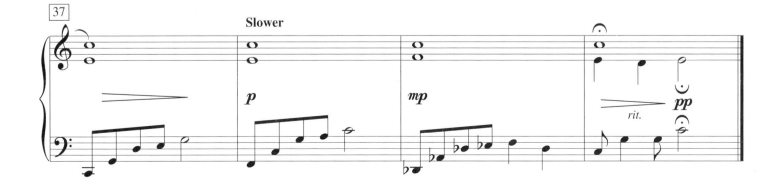

BIOGRAPHY

Randall Hartsell began his music career as a piano performance and pedagogy major at East Carolina University, but his attention turned quickly to the joys of piano composition. His childhood years in the idyllic state of North Carolina provided abundant inspiration for his trademark lyrical, romantic pieces. More recently, his music has expanded beyond the expressive melodies to also include more advanced and technically demanding compositions as well as clever and creative elementary pieces.

Workshops by Mr. Hartsell center on helping teachers foster creativity, interest in composition, developing ease in improvisation, and in polishing other essential technical skills.

His extensive involvement as music director of a Lutheran church resulted in the production of multiple arrangements and compositions of Christmas, hymn, and wedding themes. Mr. Hartsell has contributed and been featured in *Clavier Companion*, and he judges frequently for local composition contests and for the National Guild of Piano Teachers composition division. He is a past adjunct faculty member of Pfeiffer University and the University of North Carolina at Charlotte.

As a teacher, performer, composer, and church musician, Mr. Hartsell brings a wide range of experiences that enrich the lives of students and teachers.